BENJY and the BELSNICKEL

STUDY GUIDE

BENJY AND THE BELSNICKEL STUDY GUIDE

Published byWhiteSpark Publishing, a division of WhiteFire Publishing
13607 Bedford Rd NE
Cumberland, MD 21502
www.WhiteSpark-Publishing.com

Cover design by Roseanna White Designs
Cover images from Shutterstock
Interior illustrations by Xoë White

ISBNs:
      978-1-946531-82-7 (digital)
      978-1-946531-81-0 (print)

A Note to Parents and Educators

This study guide is designed to provide help in using the book, *Benjy and the Belsnickel,* as an aid in education. It contains 14 lesson plans, one for each chapter of the book. The answers for the questions in this book can either be written directly into this guide, or you can have your student use a separate notebook.

Each chapter contains a list of ten vocabulary words to help children learn the meaning of new words. Depending on your child's dictionary and research skills, you may want to discuss the meaning of the words with him. Review with your child how to write a complete sentence as that is one of the tasks he will be asked to do to answer the questions about the story.

Following the vocabulary review will be comprehension questions about what they have read in *Benjy and the Belsnickel.*

In addition to the comprehension questions, there is a section of discussion questions that parents or educators can use to motivate the child to think about why certain things occurred the way they did in the story. This is a great opportunity to interact with your child and get them to think beyond what is written in the text of the book.

A section called "Learning More" contains activities for your child to do. Many of these activities would be fun for you and your child to do together. A wide range of suggestions are presented and will further enhance what they have learned about the time period of Benjy's story. This section often contains links to helpful websites that your child can look up with your permission.

The final section provides a Bible verse that is relevant to the chapter's lesson. Encourage your child to use his or her own Bible. The purpose of this section is to create a discussion between parent and child or educator and child about how the Bible verse relates to Benjy's life.

It is our hope that you and your child will enjoy the activities in this study guide and the book, *Benjy and the Belsnickel.*

About the Author

Bonnie Swinehart grew up in Central Pennsylvania among the Pennsylvania Dutch people. Early in her career as a journalist she attended an open-house session where the Belsnickel "made an appearance." Swinehart was fascinated by the folklore behind the Belsnickel that was brought from Germany to Pennsylvania by her ancestors.

In addition, Swinehart's parents who grew up in the 1930s and attended one-room schoolhouses often spoke of their school days. Captivated with these tales, Swinehart combined the folklore surrounding the Belsnickel with children who grew up in that time period for her first book, *Benjy and the Belsnickel.*

Writing for children is a joy that Swinehart has come to love. Her first book fulfills a lifelong dream of hers to write and publish a book for children.

Benjy and the Belsnickel brings Pennsylvania Dutch folklore to life and is filled with suspense, humor, and everyday life-experiences.

Chapter One

Read pages 1-14

A B C VOCABULARY – Use a dictionary to find the meaning of these words:

schoolmarm (p. 1)

prank (p. 2)

scurried (p. 3)

woodstove (p.4)

cloakroom (p. 4)

smug (p. 5)

dunce (p. 6)

quivered (p. 9)

folklore (p. 10)

scheming (p. 11)

Use 5 of the above vocabulary words in complete sentences. Underline the vocabulary word you use. Example: Toby hung his coat in the <u>cloakroom</u>.

 COMPREHENSION

Please answer the following questions in complete sentences.

1. Who is the main character in the book? List 3 words that describe Benjy.

2. What prank did Benjy play on Miss Nettie? How do you feel about what he did?

3. Why does Benjy daydream in class?

4. What does Benjy call the woods he takes a shortcut through on his way home from school? Why?

5. Who is Benjy's fishing buddy? What language does he speak?

6. What do Benjy's parents do for a living?

DISCUSSION

1. Why did Miss Nettie make Benjy wear the dunce hat? Discuss with your teacher how you feel about the dunce hat.

2. What year does this story takes place? Discuss how a one-room schoolhouse compares to where you are taught.

3. Discuss how Benjy feels about Miss Nettie's note. What do you think will happen next?

🌐 LEARNING MORE!

▸ Draw a picture of Benjy's one room schoolhouse. Draw a picture of where you do your schoolwork. Compare the two drawings. How are they the same? Different?

▸ Ask your parents or grandparents if they know anyone who attended a one room schoolhouse. If possible, visit a one room schoolhouse. Take a picture to share with others.

▸ In what country did the story of the Belsnickel originate? How did Benjy feel about the Belsnickel? Visit the following websites and write about something you learned.

http://bit.ly/BelsnickelWiki   http://bit.ly/BelsnickelHistory

▸ Record yourself saying the Pledge of Allegiance. Visit http://ipledgeallegiance.com/

📖 BIBLE REFERENCE

Matthew 6:9

Look up Matthew 6:9 in your Bible. Discuss the Lord's Prayer.

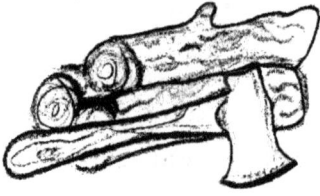

Chapter Two

Read pages 15-25

A B C **VOCABULARY** – Use a dictionary to find the meaning of these words:

gruff (p. 16)

sauntered (p. 18)

sloshing (p. 19)

tongue-lashing (p. 20)

grimaced (p. 20)

undermine (p. 21)

ornery (p. 22)

plodded (p. 23)

hightailed (p. 23)

guttural (p. 24)

Use two of the above vocabulary words to make a complete sentence. Underline the vocabulary words you use. Example: Toby's <u>ornery</u> behavior brought about a <u>tongue-lashing</u> from his father.

Use three of the above vocabulary words to write a short paragraph. Underline the vocabulary words you use.

COMPREHENSION

Please answer the following questions in complete sentences.

1. Who is Benjy's best friend? Where did Benjy find him?

2. What chore does Pop add to Benjy's list of chores as punishment for his behavior in school? Why did Pop pick that particular chore?

3. What does Benjy's pop forbid him to do as part of his punishment?

4. Benjy lives on a farm and has certain chores to do. List three of them.

5. What does Ma tell Benjy to do before bedtime?

DISCUSSION

1. Why do you think Miss Nettie stopped by Benjy's house to talk to his ma and pop?

2. How does Miss Nettie describe Benjy in the note she sends home to his parents?

3. Why does Benjy pray before falling asleep that night?

4. How does Benjy help with the garden? Why do you think a garden is important to Benjy's family?

LEARNING MORE!

▸ Benjy raises chickens. Ask your parents if it's possible to take a visit to a farm. Search the internet or try visiting the following websites and tell someone about something you learned.

> http://bit.ly/BenjyChickens1   http://bit.ly/BenjyChickens2

▸ On page 24, Benjy imagines he sees a body, arms, and long spindly fingers. What does Benjy really see? Why do you think he imagines those things?

▸ Draw a picture of Benjy's favorite meal and label it. Draw a picture of your favorite meal and label it.

BIBLE REFERENCE

Galatians 6:9

> *And let us not get tired of doing what is right, for after a while we will reap a harvest blessing if we don't get discouraged and give up.* (TLB)

> *And let us not be weary in well doing; for in due season we shall reap, if we faint not.* (KJV)

Use your Bible to look up Galatians 6:9. How do you think it might apply to Benjy?

Chapter Three

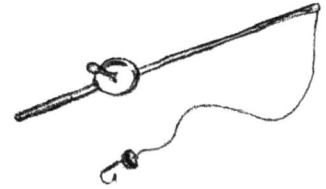

Read pages 27-39

ABC VOCABULARY – Use a dictionary to find the meaning of these words:

gawked (p. 27)

haphazardly (p. 27)

callouses (p. 29)

intently (p. 31)

plopped (p. 32)

perched (p. 36)

britches (p. 37)

eerie (p. 38)

downright (p. 38)

attuned (p. 39)

Use the vocabulary words above to fill in the blanks in each sentence with the correct word.

He looked _____ at the puzzle pieces before choosing the right one.

The shadows created an _____ sight.

I worked so hard raking the grass I got _____ on my hands.

Toby _____ at the picture of the bear hanging on the wall.

The cat was _____ to every sound heard in the basement.

I watched the owl _____ on the tree limb.

James _____ the armful of firewood inside the woodshed.

She looked _____ disgusted after losing the race.

David had a hard time choosing which _____ to wear to school.

The toys were scattered _____ across the floor.

COMPREHENSION

Please answer the following questions in complete sentences.

1. What was Benjy thinking as he struck each piece of wood with the axe?

2. Why was Pop proud of Benjy?

3. What is Benjy's nighttime prayer?

4. What did Benjy think about the new girl in his class?

DISCUSSION

1. Why did Benjy, tired and in pain from splitting wood, keep working at the chore?

2. When Benjy asks Pop if he can go fishing after completing all his chores, why did he feel guilty? What did he confess to Old Albert?

3. What happened to Benjy's voice when he tried to introduce himself to Sarah? Why did this happen?

4. How does Old Albert describe the Belsnickel to Benjy at the fishing hole? How did it affect Benjy on his trip home through Sherwood Forest?

LEARNING MORE!

▸ On one side of the line below, list the chores you do at home. On the other side, list chores that Benjy might do on the farm. Compare the two lists. Whose chores would you rather do, yours or Benjy's?

My Chores	Benjy's Chores

▸ The author describes what Benjy is thinking when he refuses to ask Pop how long he would have to chop wood. Draw a picture of Benjy's face that shows how he is feeling.

➤ Benjy catches two kinds of fish. Search the Internet for more information or try visiting the websites below to see pictures of a yellow sunfish and a silvery (white) bass. In the diagram below, draw and color a picture of each type of fish, one in each outer part of the circles. In the middle section, list how these fish are the same. Search the internet for more information.

http://bit.ly/BenjyFish1   http://bit.ly/BenjyFish2

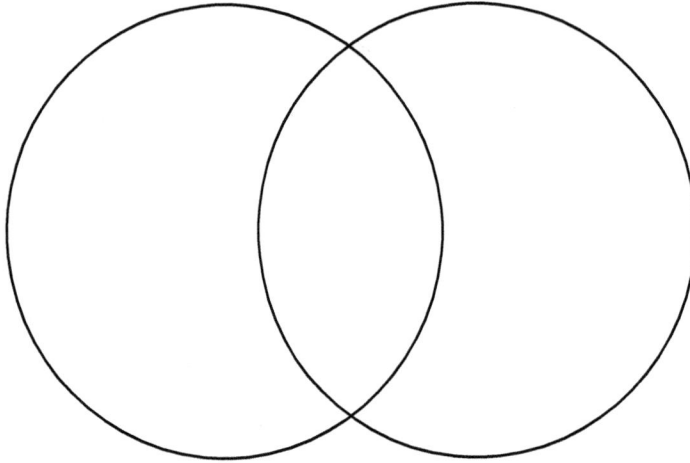

BIBLE REFERENCE

Isaiah 41:10

Fear not, for I am with you. Do not be dismayed. I am your God. I will strengthen you and I will help you. I will uphold you with my victorious right hand. (TLB)

Fear thou not; for I am with thee: be not dismayed; for I am thy God: I will strengthen thee; yea, I will uphold thee with the right hand of my righteousness. (KJV)

Use your Bible to look up Isaiah 41:10. How do you think it relates to Benjy's nighttime prayer?

Chapter Four

Read pages 41-52

ABC VOCABULARY – Use a dictionary to find the meaning of these words:

exhilaration (p. 42)

yearned (p. 43)

shifting (p. 44)

chanting (p. 44)

shimmied (p. 45)

scowled (p. 46)

uttered (p. 48)

unbar (p. 50)

frenzy (p. 51)

bustled (p. 51)

Draw a line to connect the word to its definition.

yearned	moved effortlessly
unbar	changing direction
shimmied	longed for something
exhilaration	moved excitedly
frenzy	repeating in a singsong tone
shifting	unlock
uttered	angry expression
bustled	wild behavior
scowled	made (a sound) with one's voice
chanting	a feeling of excitement

COMPREHENSION

Please answer the following questions in complete sentences.

1. What did Benjy want to do instead of sitting in the classroom?

2. Which three friends did Benjy rely on for help?

3. What playground activity did Miss Nettie do with the girls during recess?

4. How did Benjy lock the school door?

5. How did Benjy hide his chuckle from Miss Nettie? Why?

✈ DISCUSSION

1. What was Sarah's reaction when she saw Benjy jump from the window? Why?

2. What did Miss Nettie do with her students after she found herself locked out of the schoolhouse? How did the students react?

3. What word did Miss Nettie ask Benjy to spell? Why do you think she chose this word for Benjy?

4. How did Miss Nettie get the school door open? Do you think Miss Nettie knew it was Benjy and his friends who played the prank? How did she know?

🌐 LEARNING MORE!

▸ Using the 6 main characters in the chapter, color in the pie chart with red for how many were guilty of pulling the prank. Color with blue how many were innocent.

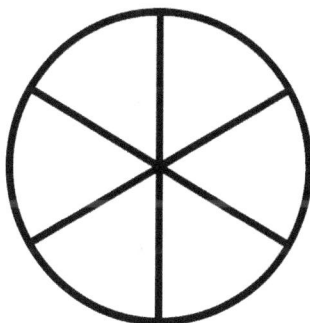

▸ What section of the chart equals 4/6 or 2/3? Which section equals 2/6 or 1/3?

▸ Draw a picture of the sport Benjy pretended to play before his friends arrived for school? Then draw a picture of your favorite sport.

▸ Search the internet for information about jump ropes. Try visiting http://bit.ly/BenjyJumpRope. Share some things you learn about jumping rope.

📖 BIBLE REFERENCE

Psalm 32:8

I will instruct you and guide you along the best pathway for your life, I will advise you and watch your progress. (TLB)

I will instruct thee and teach thee in the way which thou shalt go: I will guide thee with mine eye. (KJV)

Why might Benjy have made a different decision if he had looked to God for guidance? Do you think he would have changed his mind about his prank? Why or why not?

Chapter Five

Read pages 53-65

ABC VOCABULARY – Use a dictionary to find the meaning of these words:

maneuvered (p. 53)

alongside (p. 53)

eave (p. 54)

officially (p. 55)

reined (p. 56)

slithered (p. 58)

uneasy (p. 62)

fussed (p. 63)

focusing (p. 64)

pondered (p. 64)

Find a synonym (a word that means the same and can be substituted for the vocabulary word when used in a sentence) for each of the vocabulary words below. Search a dictionary or use a thesaurus if needed.

thought _____   troubled _____

concentrating _____   overhang _____

moved _____   annoyed_____

beside _____   slid _____

formally _____   guided _____

COMPREHENSION

Please answer the following questions in complete sentences.

1. What was special about this school day?

2. What kind of books did Benjy like to read? Why?

3. What did Lucy find in her desk when she reached for her book report? How did Lucy react? Why?

4. What did the girls in the classroom do when they saw the snake?

5. What kind of lesson did Miss Nettie teach the children while holding the snake?

6. Where did the snake go after Miss Nettie was done teaching her lesson? Why?

 DISCUSSION

1. How did Miss Nettie get to school in chapter five? How did she learn to ride it? How could the children benefit from this advice?

2. Benjy quickly chose two books from the library cart. What kind of books do you like to read? Why?

3. What kind of snake did Lucy find in her desk? Describe how it looked.

4. Why do you think Miss Nettie named the snake Belsnickel?

 LEARNING MORE!

➤ On your own paper, write two or three paragraphs about your favorite book.

➤ Search the internet or visit http://bit.ly/BenjySnakes to learn more about garter snakes. List two more things you learned about garter snakes after you searched for information.

➤ Fold a piece of 8 x 11 paper in half two times. You should have four sections. In each section, write a reason why libraries are important to students. On this scale from 1 to 10, circle the number that shows how you feel about your library, where 1 is "I don't like it at all" and 10 is "I love it!"

1 2 3 4 5 6 7 8 9 10

 BIBLE REFERENCE

Psalm 94:19

Lord, when doubts fill my mind, when my heart is in turmoil, quiet me and give me renewed hope and cheer. (TLB)

In the multitude of my thoughts within me thy comforts delight my soul. (KJV)

Use your Bible to look up Psalm 94:19. In Benjy's prayer, he feels there is no hope for himself. How might he feel after reading this verse?

Chapter Six

Read pages 67-83

ABC VOCABULARY – Use a dictionary to find the meaning of these words:

buttery (p. 68)

reaction (p. 69)

riffle (p. 70)

nippy (p. 71)

penmanship (p. 73)

equation (p. 74)

handkerchief (p. 77)

dribbled (p. 78)

composure (p. 79)

shuddered (p. 82)

Place your vocabulary words in the correct columns. If needed, search for the words in chapter six, use the internet, or look them up in a dictionary.

<u>Nouns</u>   <u>Verbs</u>   <u>Adjectives</u>

COMPREHENSION

Please answer the following questions in complete sentences.

1. Who was the special guest coming to visit the school? Why was he there?

2. What three things did everyone eat for lunch that day?

3. Why did Benjy quickly pull something from his desk when Miss Nettie came around to inspect it?

4. From what type of book did Benjy have to read in front of the class? Why?

5. Why did Mr. Lewis yell for water? How much water did he need?

6. Why did Miss Nettie give Benjy another warning about the Belsnickel?

✈ DISCUSSION

1. Why did Benjy dump the pepper into Mr. Lewis' soup? Do you think his prank worked? Why or why not?

2. What kind of chores did the students have to do to get the schoolhouse ready for Mr. Lewis' visit? What kind of chores do you help with at your school or teaching area?

3. Discuss the punishment Benjy received. Would a teacher use that kind of punishment today? Why or why not?

4. What kind of rating do you think Mr. Lewis gave the school after Benjy pulled his prank?

🌐 LEARNING MORE!

➤ Invite a group of friends or family to play the game "Mother May I" or draw a picture of Benjy and his friends playing the game. Look for game instructions online or visit the web at http://bit.ly/BenjyGame.

➤ With supervision, bake some sugar cookies like Sarah baked. Follow a favorite family recipe or search for a recipe on the internet. Try visiting http://bit.ly/BenjyCookies and watch the short video.

➤ Compare the lunch you were served today to a lunch the children were served at Benjy's school. Make two lists, one with the things you ate today and one with the things the children ate at school (pages 68 and 69) in this chapter. Which lunch sounds better? Which lunch sounds healthier? Draw a happy face on the list that has the lunch you would rather eat.

My Lunch	Benjy's Lunch

➤ Benjy came to dislike the sound of a jingle bell. Why? Place a jingle bell on your dresser or nightstand to remind yourself to always choose good behavior.

📖 BIBLE REFERENCE

James 1:5

If you want to know what God wants you to do, ask him, and he will gladly tell you, for he is always ready to give a bountiful supply of wisdom to all who ask; he will not resent it. (TLB)

If any of you lack wisdom, let him ask of God, that giveth to all men liberally, and upbraidith not; and it shall be given him. (KJV)

Look up James 1:5 in your Bible. Benjy seems to make some bad decisions. Do you? How can this verse help everyone make better decisions?

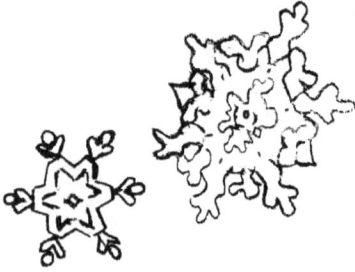

Chapter Seven

Read pages 85-99

ABC VOCABULARY – Use a dictionary to find the meaning of these words:

generously (p. 86)

burlap (p. 87)

system (p. 88)

overtook (p.89)

stoke (p. 89)

tampered (p. 92)

diphtheria (p. 93)

venture (p. 95)

disentangled (p. 96)

barbed (p. 96)

Using the above vocabulary words, unscramble the words below. Example: tnwire - <u>winter</u>

uetnrve _____   ndtaeesilndg _____

rotokveo _____   puarlb _____

ebdbra _____   oekts _____

selgeoynru _____   ipradheiht _____

epramdte _____   mtsesy _____

COMPREHENSION

Please answer the following questions in complete sentences.

1. What was the name of the place where Benjy and his friends went sledding? Who owned the land?

2. Who did Benjy have to beat to the schoolhouse in the morning in order for his prank to work? Why?

3. What kind of prank did Benjy pull in this chapter?

4. Why did Miss Nettie have to send all the children home upon their arrival at school?

5. Who rode in the bobsled on its first run down the hill? Would you like to ride on a bobsled? Tell why.

6. What happened to Joshua while sledding?

DISCUSSION

1. Discuss with your teacher how Benjy prevented the woodstove's smoke from going up the chimney.

2. What different kinds of sleds did the children use at Dorsey Hill? What type of sleds do children use today? Which is your favorite?

3. What did Benjy do to help Joshua when he got injured? Discuss what you would do if you had to help a friend who got hurt or tell about a time when you actually did help someone.

LEARNING MORE!

➤ Look on the internet to find out what Balto the Sled Dog did to help someone. What kind of dog was he? Look for and draw a picture of Balto.

➤ In this chapter Benjy walked through a big snowstorm. Make paper snowflakes by searching the internet for patterns or visit http://bit.ly/BenjySnowflakes for help. Write your vocabulary words on the snowflakes.

➤ In this chapter, you read about Lightning Guider sleds. These sleds were made in Duncannon, PA, at The Old Sled Works, a building that has been turned into an antique mall with a little sled museum. Visit the museum or visit http://bit.ly/BenjySledMarker. Read the marker and write something you learned about Lightning Guider sleds.

BIBLE REFERENCE

Galatians 6:2

> *Share each other's troubles and problems, and so obey our Lord's command.* (TLB)

> *Bear ye one another's burdens, and so fulfill the law of Christ.* (KJV)

Use your Bible to look up Galatians 6:2. How did Benjy fulfill this verse in this chapter?

Chapter Eight

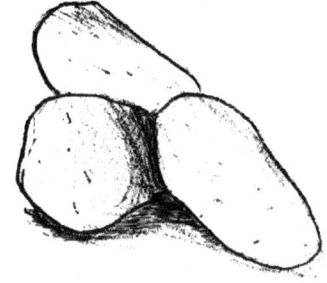

Read pages 101-115

ABC VOCABULARY – Use a dictionary to find the meaning of these words:

savory (p. 103)

tantalizing (p. 103)

flailed (p. 104)

sidestepped (p. 105)

bearings (p. 105)

foreboding (p. 106)

perimeter (p. 108)

fidgeted (p. 108)

remorse (p. 114)

scrawny (p. 114)

Choose the best answers to each question below. Circle the correct answer.

1. Which is the most tantalizing to you?

    a. math test

    b. old sneaker

    c. chocolate cake

    d. roll of tape

2. What is the most foreboding?

    a. old creepy house

    b. Christmas tree

    c. cuckoo clock

    d. flowers

3. What is the opposite of remorse?

    a. regret

    b. sadness

    c. sorrow

    d. contentment

4. Which is most likely to be flailed?

    a. ice cream

    b. cardboard box

    c. sword

    d. kitten

COMPREHENSION

Please answer the following questions in complete sentences.

1. What special event did Benjy look forward to in this chapter? What activity did the children do during the event?

2. Why did Benjy's mother send him to the ground cellar?

3. What did Benjy hear while in the ground cellar? Do you think the sound was real or part of Benjy's imagination? Why?

4. What was Old Albert doing when Benjy arrived at the barn dance?

5. What new character did the author introduce in this chapter?

DISCUSSION

1. How did Sarah react when Benjy pointed to the dance floor? Discuss why you think Sarah responded the way she did.

2. Discuss how Benjy reacted when his friends asked him what he wanted for Christmas. Why did he react this way?

3. Discuss Benjy's dream. Why do you think this dream scared him?

LEARNING MORE!

▸ What did the children have to do before pulling the taffy? How long did they have to pull the taffy? Search the Internet or visit http://bit.ly/BenjyTaffy for a taffy recipe. If possible, have a taffy pulling party.

▸ What is a ground cellar used for? Name some things you would find in a ground or root cellar. Visit http://bit.ly/BenjyRootCellar to learn how to build a simple ground or root cellar today.

▸ While baking, Benjy's mother hums Christmas songs. Pick your favorite Christmas song and record yourself singing it, or sing it to a family member or with a friend. Why is this song your favorite?

BIBLE REFERENCE

Psalm 46:1

> *God is our refuge and strength, a tested help in times of trouble.* (TLB)

> *God is our refuge and strength, a very present help in trouble.* (KJV)

Look up Psalm 46:1 in your Bible. At the end of Chapter Eight, Benjy crawls under the covers and snuggles up with Mutt. Why? How does this verse provide Benjy with the protection he yearns for?

Chapter Nine

Read pages 117-130

A B C VOCABULARY – Use a dictionary to find the meaning of these words:

zestful (p. 117)

ushered (p. 117)

quest (p. 118)

upright (p. 120)

hubbub (p. 121)

scrawled (p.121)

vigorously (p. 122)

rummaged (p. 122)

baffled (p. 123)

disgruntled (123)

Put the above vocabulary words in alphabetical order. Use five of the words in a paragraph.

1.   6.

2.   7.

3.   8.

4.   9.

5.   10.

COMPREHENSION

Please answer the following questions in complete sentences.

1. What did Miss Nettie want the children to find on their quest?

2. Why did Benjy think the Belsnickel was spying on him in the woods?

3. Who found the perfect tree for the schoolroom? What kind of tree was it?

4. What did Miss Nettie pull from her desk drawer? Why did she need this?

5. Why does the storekeeper get disgruntled with Benjy?

✈ DISCUSSION

1. Discuss why Benjy turned to his ma for help in picking out a present for Sarah. Who would you ask to help you if you weren't sure what present to get a special person?

2. In this chapter Benjy broke a promise to his mother. How did he feel? Discuss how you would feel if you failed someone who was counting on you.

3. Discuss why Benjy came to Sarah's rescue during the snowball fight.

4. Why did Miss Nettie tell the children not to tell anyone whose name they drew in the gift exchange?

🌐 LEARNING MORE!

➤ If possible, go to a Christmas tree farm this year and choose your own tree. Like Benjy, you may be able to help chop or saw down the tree with supervision.

➤ Try using recycled paper to make a paper chain Christmas tree. Visit http://bit.ly/BenjyPaperChain to get directions. Take a picture of your tree to share with others.

➤ *Grischdaag* is Pennsylvania Dutch for "Christmas." Use the internet to look up the Pennsylvania Dutch word for "tree." Now write a sentence using both Pennsylvania Dutch words.

➤ On one side of the line below, list what the children in chapter nine did during indoor recess. On the other side, list the things you and your friends do during indoor recess. Place a sticker or draw a star on the list that sounds like more fun. Tell someone why that list of things to do is more fun.

My Recess	Benjy's Recess

📖 BIBLE REFERENCE

John 15:11

> *I have told you this so that you may be filled with my joy. Yes, your cup of joy will overflow.* (TLB)

> *These things I have spoken unto you, that my joy might remain in you, and that your joy might be full.* (KJV)

Look up John 15:11 in your Bible. What made the children joyful as they prepared for Christmas?

Chapter Ten

Read pages 131-143

ABC VOCABULARY – Use a dictionary to find the meaning of these words:

peered (p. 131)

traditions (p. 131)

shawl (p. 132)

unbearable (p. 133)

erupted (p. 134)

sheepishly (p.134)

whittled (p. 136)

glistening (p. 136)

nestled (p. 141)

reality (p. 141)

Use the vocabulary words above to fill in the blanks in each sentence with the correct word.

Ruth wore a _____ to keep herself warm.

Samuel didn't know if it was a dream or _____.

Christopher _____ a piece of wood into the shape of a cow.

The pain was almost _____ after Robert cut his finger.

The kittens were all _____ together in a basket.

Betty _____ over top of her mother's shoulder.

The volcano _____ late into the night.

What are your family's favorite holiday _____?

The light shining on the snow had a _____ effect.

Toby _____ got caught with a piece of candy.

COMPREHENSION

Please answer the following questions in complete sentences.

1. What tradition did Benjy and his ma enjoy doing together?

2. What was Benjy supposed to get for his ma at the store? Why?

3. What did Benjy get in the gift exchange? Who was he going to ask for help in playing a tune?

4. What kind of presents did Miss Nettie receive from her students?

5. Why did Benjy keep looking out the window at the snowstorm? Why was he worried?

6. How did church affect Benjy's nerves?

DISCUSSION

1. Discuss the gift Benjy chose for Sarah. Why did he choose that particular gift? What was Sarah's reaction when opening her present?

2. What did Pop tell Benjy as they were getting the horses hooked to the sleigh? How do you think Benjy felt?

3. Discuss why Benjy sank down into the straw on the way home from church. How was he feeling? Have you ever felt this way? What did you do?

LEARNING MORE!

▸ On Christmas Eve, the parishioners acted out the Nativity. Using your own nativity scene or drawing, tell the nativity story to a younger child.

▸ Use craft foam and/or colored felt to make gingerbread man decorations to hang on your tree or make cinnamon and applesauce gingerbread ornaments from http://bit.ly/BenjyOrnaments.

▸ If you live where someone provides sleigh rides, plan to take one. If not, make a snow collage from magazine or internet photos.

▸ With a group of friends and family, sing Benjy's favorite Christmas hymn, "Silent Night." If you play an instrument, join in with the music.

BIBLE REFERENCE

Matthew 1:21

> *And she will have a Son, and you are to give him the name Jesus, for he will save his people from their sins.* (TLB)

> *And she shall bring forth a son, and thou shalt call his name JESUS: for he shall save his people from their sins.* (KJV)

Look up Matthew 1:21 in your Bible. Discuss the purpose of Jesus' birth.

Chapter Eleven

Read pages 145-154

ABC VOCABULARY – Use a dictionary to find the meaning of these words:

refuge (p. 145)

jittery (p. 146)

fitful (p. 146)

menacing (p.147)

collided (p. 149)

malicious (p. 150)

fiery (p. 152)

tirade (p. 153)

chortled (p. 154)

cackle (p. 154)

For each of the underlined words in the sentences below, choose the word in parenthesis that is an antonym (a word that means the opposite). If you need help, check a dictionary or a thesaurus. Example: Toby wore a hideous mask. (ugly or pretty)

He ran from the pouring rain toward <u>refuge</u> in the cave. (danger or shelter)

Susan's hands felt <u>jittery</u> as she waited for John to arrive. (nervous or calm)

Benjy had a <u>fitful</u> night's sleep. (peaceful or disturbing)

The dream was <u>menacing</u>. (scary or friendly)

Kenny's car <u>collided</u> against the tree. (missed or banged)

Betty wore a <u>malicious</u> grin. (friendly or unfriendly)

She had a <u>fiery</u> disposition. (gentle or angry)

The crowd was in a <u>tirade</u> after the show. (yelling mood or talking mood)

The woman <u>chortled</u> with delight. (whispered or laughed)

Sam heard the old man <u>cackle</u>. (loud cry or silent cry)

COMPREHENSION

Please answer the following questions in complete sentences.

1. Who were Buckwheat and Clover? What did they do on Christmas Eve?

2. Why did Benjy have a hard time sleeping?

3. What happened when Benjy opened the parlor door? Why did that happen?

4. What did Benjy take along downstairs to protect himself?

5. What was written on the Belsnickel's ragged paper scroll?

✈ DISCUSSION

1. Why was Benjy scared to answer the *rap, rap, rap,* he heard at the parlor door? What did he think would happen?

2. How many misbehaviors did the Belsnickel have written on his scroll? Discuss at least three of these. Which one do you think was the worst? Why?

3. Discuss why the Belsnickel tossed some candies toward Benjy before he left the house?

🌐 LEARNING MORE!

▸ Draw a picture of the Belsnickel hat. Label the details you drew.

▸ You will need crayons or colored pencils to complete the activity on the scale below. Rank how scared you think Benjy was in this chapter. The number one means not scared at all. Number ten means very scared. (1) Using green, circle the number on the scale to show how scared you think Benjy was before he went to bed that night. (2) Using red, circle the number to show how scared you think Benjy was when the Belsnickel cracked the whip. (3) Using blue, circle the number to show how scared you think Benjy was when the Belsnickel left the house.

1   2   3   4   5   6   7   8   9   10

▸ Fold a piece of paper in half. On one side list some of the good things you've done. On the other side list some of the naughty things you've done.

📖 BIBLE REFERENCE

Psalms 86:5

> *O Lord, you are so good and kind, so ready to forgive; so full of mercy for all who ask your aid.* (TLB)

> *For thou, Lord, art good, and ready to forgive; and plenteous in mercy unto all them that call upon thee.* (KJV)

Look up Psalms 86:5 in your Bible. Benjy makes a promise to the Belsnickel to do better. Discuss how he can be assured that his prior pranks or misbehaviors can be forgiven.

Chapter Twelve

Read pages 155-170

ABC VOCABULARY – Use a dictionary to find the meaning of these words:

pesky (p. 155)

whiff (p. 156)

aside (p. 157)

gripping (p. 158)

hearty (p. 159)

slung (p. 161)

traipse (p. 163)

churned (p. 164)

clacking (p. 166)

horizon (p. 167)

Using the above vocabulary words, draw a line to match the word to the correct definition.

slung	walk aimlessly
churned	a short distance apart
gripping	annoying
horizon	tossed
whiff	holding firmly
clacking	moved or shook
pesky	exuberant
traipse	smell
hearty	the line between earth and sky
aside	quick, sharp sound

COMPREHENSION

Please answer the following questions in complete sentences.

1. Where did Benjy stash his nuts and candies? Why did he stash them there?

2. What did Benjy find in his stocking?

3. How did Benjy find his present under the Christmas tree?

4. Who was Benjy's lunch guest? What did he bring with him?

5. What did Mrs. Perkins put in Sarah's and Benjy's coat pockets? Why did she do this?

6. Who challenged Benjy and his friends to a hockey game? Why did they challenge Benjy and his friends to a game?

DISCUSSION

1. Horsewhip or candies—why did Benjy think the Belsnickel gave him a choice between the two?

2. What did Benjy get for Christmas? Do you think he deserved to get a present? Why or why not?

3. How would you describe Bruce Yeager?

4. Benjy had a tough decision to make between staying for the hockey game or walking Sarah home like he promised. Did Benjy make the right decision? Explain why you think this.

LEARNING MORE!

> Draw a picture of a hockey stick used today. Draw a picture of the hockey sticks Benjy and his teammates used. Compare the two drawings. How are they different? Same?

> With your friends, plan a visit to an indoor ice-skating rink for an afternoon of fun.

> Ask your grandparents or a resident of a retirement home what their Christmas was like as a child. Search the internet for information on Christmas in the 1930s or visit http://bit.ly/Benjy1930s.

BIBLE REFERENCE

2 Corinthians 9:7

> *Every one must make up his own mind as to how much he should give. Don't force anyone to give more than he really wants to, for cheerful givers are the ones God prizes.* (TLB)

> *Every man according as he purposeth in his heart, so let him give; not grudgingly, or of necessity; for God loveth a cheerful giver.* (KJV)

Look up 2 Corinthians 9:7 in your Bible. What does this verse say about cheerful givers? Are you a cheerful giver?

Chapter Thirteen

Read pages 171-182

A B C VOCABULARY – Use a dictionary to find the meaning of these words:

normally (p. 172)

drifted (p. 172)

assured (p. 174)

erect (p. 174)

clammy (p. 175)

hurling (p. 176)

speckled (p. 177)

smirked (p. 178)

excess (p. 178)

retrieve (p. 180)

Choose the best answers to each question below. Circle the correct answer.

1. Which would be clammy?

    a. sand castle

    b. birthday card

    c. book

    d. sweaty hand

2. What is the most erect?

    a. sleeping child

    b. a saluting soldier

    c. blanket

    d. wilted plant

3. What is the opposite of retrieve?

    a. let go

    b. bring back

    c. lose

    d. send away

4. Which is most likely to be hurling?

    a. ruler

    b. kitchen table

    c. baseball player

    d. school desk

COMPREHENSION

Please answer the following questions in complete sentences.

1. What special day occurred in this chapter? How many children participated?

2. Who did Miss Nettie put in charge of making the card box?

3. Why did the children have to keep quiet? What were they told to do?

4. What grade did Benjy get on his test paper? How did he feel about that grade? How would you feel?

5. What special treat did the children help to make for their party?

6. What did Miss Nettie give each student on this special day?

DISCUSSION

1. Why does Miss Nettie make such a big deal about Valentine's Day?

2. What did Benjy admit to Ma while making a valentine for Sarah? Do you think Ma already new about his feelings? Why?

3. Who did Benjy hope would know about his good test score? Why?

LEARNING MORE!

▸ On a snowy day, gather your friends together to play a game of "Being Measured." Reread pages 175-176 in your book to remember how it is played. Could you play this game with crinkled balls of paper if there is no snow on the ground? What else could you use? Give it a try!

▸ Make valentine cards for your friends and family even if it's not Valentine's Day. You can save them to give next year.

▸ With help from an adult and lots of friends, make some ice cream with a hand-turned crank, if you have one available. (Besides the ice cream ingredients, you will also need an ice cream freezer, ice, snow, and rock salt.) Or else search the web for a picture of one or visit http://bit.ly/BenjyIceCream. Draw a picture of the children at Benjy's school cranking the ice cream in Chapter Thirteen.

BIBLE REFERENCE

Ephesians 5:1

Follow God's example in everything you do just as a much loved child imitates his father. (TLB)

Be ye therefore followers of God, as dear children. (KJV)

Look up Ephesians 5:1 in your Bible. Chapter Thirteen is a feel-good chapter with children showing love for one another and adults showing love to their children. How might this verse relate to this chapter?

Chapter Fourteen

Read pages 183-196

A B C VOCABULARY – Use a dictionary to find the meaning of these words:

accommodate (p. 185)

participate (p. 186)

representative (p. 188)

gaping (p. 188)

pronounce (p. 189)

competition (p. 191)

opponent (p. 191)

apprehension (p. 192)

permanent (p. 192)

determined (p. 193)

Find a synonym (a word that means the same and can be substituted for the vocabulary word when used in a sentence) for each of the vocabulary words below. Search a dictionary or use a thesaurus if needed.

challenger _____   join in _____

long-lasting _____   firm _____

speak _____   shelter _____

suspicion _____   wide open _____

contest _____   agent _____

COMPREHENSION

Please answer the following questions in complete sentences.

1. What sound did Benjy hear that meant spring was near?

2. What kind of homework did Miss Nettie give the students the most? Why?

3. Who did Miss Nettie choose as the sixth-grade representative in the spelling bee?

4. Why did Benjy have trouble eating breakfast the morning of the spelling bee? What did his stomach feel like?

5. With whom did Benjy share his picnic lunch?

6. What word did Benjy spell wrong in the contest?

DISCUSSION

1. Why do you think Miss Nettie chose Benjy to represent the sixth-grade class in the spelling bee? How did Benjy feel about being chosen? How would you feel?

2. Who helped Benjy practice all his spelling words? Why?

3. What noise did Benjy imagine he heard that prompted him to hurry to get to school on time? Why do you think he heard this noise in his head?

4. Why did Miss Nettie want to see Benjy in the schoolhouse after the competition? How did Benjy react?

LEARNING MORE!

On your own paper, write one or two paragraphs about your favorite part of the book.

Benjy heard the geese honking as a sign of spring. Name some other signs that spring is near.

What is a sack race and a three-legged race? Try visiting the internet at http://bit.ly/BenjyRace. Plan a race like this with your friends, but be sure to get your parents' permission.

What is the most important lesson you learned from *Benjy and the Belsnickel*?

BIBLE REFERENCE

2 Timothy 2:5

Follow the Lord's rules for doing his work, just as an athlete either follows the rules or is disqualified and wins no prize. (TLB)

And if a man also strive for masteries, yet is he not crowned, except he strive lawfully. (KJV)

Use your Bible to look up 2 Timothy 2:5. Discuss Benjy's role in the spelling bee competition and in the children's games. What does this verse tell us about competing?